JOURNEY INTO POETRY

"Composition with Old Wood" by Stephen T. Vessels

Journey into Poetry

Lynn Hoins and Chloé McFeters

60 Poems in 30 Days

SHERMAN POINT
PRESS

To

My daughter, Mickey Nowicki-Clark.
You light up my life every day.

Lynn Hoins

and

Heather Lyn, my forever friend,
and my very first writing partner.

Chloé McFeters

A true friend is somebody who can make us do what we can.
— RALPH WALDO EMERSON

...all shall be well, and all shall be well,
and all manner of things shall be well.
— JULIAN OF NORWICH, *Revelations of Divine Love*

Contents

Foreword

Long ago, when I first encountered abstract expressionism, I thought it was nonsense. I spewed stock dismissals: a kid could do that, it's a con job, etc. Years later someone said something to me that so altered my perspective I couldn't reclaim how I'd seen before. It was like walking through an invisible barrier and looking back to find the way unchanged yet entirely transformed. We stopped to look through a gallery window at a painting that consisted of a sparse, random-seeming distribution of brushstrokes in primary colors. I made a noise indicative of my disapproval, but my companion said he liked it. "Oh," I decried, with theatrical incredulity, "how is that possible?" He answered, "I can see how it was made."

> *If you really want to know,*
> *I'm thinking about things like*
> *. . . whether or not butterflies*
> *remember their former selves*
>
> – cm

The incident is significant for me in several ways. I know that it happened in Boulder, Colorado, sometime in the late 1970's, but cannot with any greater precision recall when it occurred nor whom I was with. The identity of my enlightener is lost to me. And yet I know it was that exact moment when I began a series of reflections that forever changed how I viewed art and the world.

> *Reluctant feet take first step.*
> *Fist knuckles tears away.*
>
> – lh

xiii

I no longer saw those random-seeming brushstrokes as the acts of an artist but of a human. And as such the *fact* that they had been applied became a companion consideration to the care – the precision – of their application. Intentionality did not lose its place as a criterion for appreciating a work of art, it just moved over to make room for another. I thought of paint, and brushes, and canvas, and what a miracle it is not only that any of those things exist, but that they are so abundantly available they are taken for granted. I thought about what it says about humanity that we create such things, and how it speaks well of us that we do. I never disparaged abstract expressionism again.

I wonder if your grandmother was a warrior
And whether she was haunted by ghosts

– cm

There is much to be valued in works that are so skillfully rendered it is nearly impossible to discern how they were made. Certain pastels of Edgar Degas are good examples - an expression so clear on a subject's face that their character is revealed, but when you look closely it's composed of minuscule smudges bearing no clear relation to each other. There is also a great deal to be gained from a work so transparent in its design that it seems it was easy to do. Until you put yourself in the artist's shoes and reflect on what it took to live as they lived and do what they did.

You can see where smoke
would come out of its nose
as it breathed fire.

– lh

The evolution of language is a mist over the history of consciousness. Clearly, we want to communicate; how we do so remains mysterious. Nowhere more than in writing is the road to a finished product invisible. The reader cannot see the words that were changed or deleted, which added, which phrases moved about, how something that began as one thing became another. Unless the author decides to let their blunders and falterings be seen. That's what you have in your hands, the unvarnished, unlaundered efforts of two poets composing, as it were, in the nude.

No one seems to find me here
I exist within an emptiness

– cm

The results are significant in several ways. Perhaps most in how good the poems are. How well they read, absent reexamination or amendment. As if knowing that, like the artist who sketches in ink, they had but one shot at getting it right, honed their focus, and dismissed ineptitude. In these poems can be seen not only the work but the consequence of commitment.

Day after day, month after month,
we broke open 30 oranges
with our fingernails.

– lh

Thirty poems in thirty days.

There is an occasional phrase not quite as well hewn as it might have been with further thought, a skip in cadence, an unneeded trope. I can sense the drag to the desk, of a day, to check off the obligation. The crush, of another day, to get something neither fully formed nor understood said.

I'm super dynamic
I keep things interesting
And I'm always on the move.

– cm

I can feel the frustration, smell the bitterness. Life is going on in the background. No, that's wrong: these lines were written in the middles of lives. They are immersed in honeyed sufferings and sour beauties. In one place a trivial delight is exalted, in another mortality sits down and puts up its feet.

Doctor said

terminal

Mind went blank

– lh

The Inclination to examine, criticize, reassess, alter is itself laid bare to question. The *fact* that these words were written, one after another, and arranged as they are, is made a worthy consideration alongside the precision with which it was done. All things are finite, and one does not get to do over one's life. At what point, in what measure, beneath what sky, does the inner editor retire? Are all such decisions not to some extent arbitrary? Rhetorical questions need no answers. In the mill of millions of writers reaching for perfection, striving to extract something pure and unassailable from the language that was handed down to them, two decided to let the day's effort stand.

It was a disaster house in so many ways,

yet I learned to love it.

– lh

Herein there are no errors, for they were meant to be seen.

Stephen T. Vessels

Los Angeles, California
March 2020

Acknowledgments

This book, and our friendship, owe their existence to Susan Ariel Rainbow Kennedy, an inspiration, creative mentor, and friend to us both. We wish to thank her for her loving luminosity from the bottoms of our hearts.

The Community Writing Center of Salt Lake Community College inspired us to write these poems by offering the challenge to write 30 poems in 30 days to celebrate April, National Poetry Month. We are grateful for the provision of daily prompts to impel us to let poetry live in us daily. Their encouragement helped us remember we are poets.

We would also like to express our deepest gratitude to our editor extraordinaire, Chris Wozney, for her support, generosity, and expertise. Chris is an exceptional writer and editor, and we are fortunate to have had her guidance with this book.

Heartfelt appreciation goes to Stephen T. Vessels, whose intelligence, skill, and humor make everything better. We are honored to include his foreword and illustration, "Composition with Old Wood," in *Journey into Poetry*.

Our most sincere praise and thanks go to Richard H. Fox, Jon Sebba, Rochelle S. Cohen, Eileen Van Hook, and Louis H. Metoyer, for sharing their beautiful poetry with our readers. You are all wonderful poets and people and you bless us both with your words.

Special thanks and much love to all of those in our CC: Elizabeth, Crystal, Christy, Lindy, Betsy, Mickey, and Jen. You are beloved creative companions. We are inspired by each of you and how you show up in this world.

Our wholehearted gratitude to CK, for your unwavering love and support. You are so very loved by us both.

To our family and friends, for your encouragement and belief in us, and for all of the ways you add such joy, color, and meaning to our lives, we thank you.

And lastly, we remember Dorcas Watters, with deep gratitude for the gift of her life and words.

Preface

We first met in an online creative group and discovered that we shared a favorite place in common: a beach in a small town in New England where we had both had profound experiences. It was a lovely coincidence that formed an immediate connection across the many miles that separate us. We also learned that we shared a lot of the same loves and interests, including our love of writing and poetry. And so it was, drawn by those common interests, that we became friends for life.

In April of 2019 we combined our shared interests to work side by side on a poetry project, taking part in a "30 poems in 30 days" challenge for National Poetry Month. This book is the product of our efforts.

Even though we are both published poets, we hadn't written much poetry at that time and felt our inner poets had been asleep for too long. Neither of us had ever partnered with anyone to do anything like this, and the prospect of making the commitment together was exciting. We both like working with deadlines and know that it's often easier to meet someone else's deadline than it is to meet our own. Nevertheless, time was the biggest obstacle. Composing 30 poems in 30 days takes time and focus. Life doesn't stop to make it easier. It stretched us both to meet the daily deadline for a month. It also got us back in the groove of writing.

There were other obstacles. Some of the daily prompts we were given proved challenging for us. But we stuck with them because that was part of the commitment we'd made. We had to accept that we could only do what we could do. Expecting perfection of ourselves would have been a sure recipe for failure. We didn't have time to let our poems lie fallow so we could revisit them with fresh eyes. These poems had to be immediate, warts and all. We both experienced frustrations with the music of our words, and often felt our efforts were clunky. We called and emailed each other to see how our heads were doing after being banged, daily, against so many walls. We groaned a lot. We also laughed a lot. In spite of the difficulties, we had a great time.

Early on, we both sort of joked about how it might be fun to put our poems together and share them with family and friends. Once we'd completed the challenge, we felt that what we had done together as friends and creative companions was special. We might not have produced the greatest poetry, but we had supported each other, we had followed through with our mutual commitment, and we'd spent a month drenched in the poetic process. "I *have* to write a poem today" became "I *get* to write a poem today." That was a good feeling, one we thought might prove contagious.

We wondered if other people might enjoy taking a peek at our unedited journey, at our rough roads and not just destinations. We hoped it might encourage some to take their own journeys, that it might spark in someone else an idea for a poem or a challenge. Who could guess where that might lead?

With that hope, we decided to share our sixty somewhat rough-hewn poems. That's part of the learning process too – letting one's work be seen. We reached inward for the courage to say, "We know these poems may not be perfect, but we want others to see what it was like to knuckle down, make a commitment, and see it through."

When we pick up a published book, we don't see the time, patience, deep breaths, and sweating brows, to say nothing of the redlines of professional editors. This can create the impression that flawless work flows out of writers from the second they sit down to write. And sometimes that is undoubtedly the case. Most of the time, for most writers, it isn't. But writing is a skill and a craft that can be learned. Wherever one starts, with time and effort they will get better. We hope others will find this book to be an invitation to begin writing, maybe with someone you love and admire, who can support you and make you laugh along the way.

This Journey into Poetry was unexpected, and it was one of the most enjoyable things either of us has ever done. If this book encourages others to take their own journeys, it's worth exposing our warts along with any jewels we may have produced.

Lynn and Chloé

January 2021

The Challenge

Each morning, during the month of April, we were provided with a new prompt. Most were topic or genre-based, others pictorial. Our task was to find a way to write an original poem that would meaningfully incorporate the prompt from that day.

The total word count for all 30 poems combined could not exceed 4000 words. That was tough! For the competition, we both had to trim some poems to get our manuscripts under the word limit. In a few cases here, we have restored our poems to their original lengths.

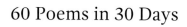

60 Poems in 30 Days

Day 1. We were asked to write a poem about breakfast.

Breakfast

Last week breakfast in bed:
delicious homemade pumpkin muffins,
oatmeal with half and half, or
cranberry orange scones.
My daughter spoiled me.

This morning, in my empty house,
I'm not hungry. I don't want
to stagger down to the kitchen
or clamber upstairs where my stash
of oatmeal hides. I dip my bright green plastic spoon
in the emergency jar of peanut butter near my bed.
Wait.

I grab my purse where four homemade
peanut butter cookies were tucked away
for the flight home.
I savor the cookies and my daughter's love.

— lh

Honest

Breakfast, I so rarely relish you.
I'm sorry.

It's not you, it's me.
Like, today for example,
you're delicious.
You really are.
You're mango sweet
and banana smooth.
You're protein
and you're healthy carbs.
You're everything
a bountiful breakfast should be,
and yet

if I'm honest,
I find myself fantasizing about
French Toast.
Four sourdough slices
soaked in butter
and vats of Vermont maple syrup.
I am drooling at the dream of bacon,
maple-smoked bacon,
two whole pieces,
and also,
selfishly,
some sausage on the side.

Breakfast,
you, as is, are mouthwatering
and beautiful,

but I so rarely taste you
or appreciate your beauty,
not even for a second.
I'm sorry.

It's just that, you see,
I get too easily distracted.
I should be focused on you
and me, I know,
on our fleeting time together,
but I'm not.
I should sit and savor the moment,
take you into me slowly
get familiar with all of your flavors
and your flavonoids,
but I don't.

I'm reading, and
I'm typing, and
if you really want to know,
I'm thinking about things like
laundry, and
shaving, and
what to make for dinner.
(I know that must hurt, but it's true.)
About whether or not butterflies
remember their former selves
inching along
and unable to fly.
About why we hurt one another,
tear each other down,
forget our own humanity.
About how many text messages
I still need to respond to
and which new shows

I can binge-watch
on Netflix.
About what kinds of kites
I might design
if ever I were a kite designer.
About the person who invented
the automatic car wash
and how ingenious they were
and how rich they must be
and yet

every morning
just like me
they need you.
We're all unable to fly, you see.
At least without you.

Sometimes
I notice that I am ignoring you
and I try,
for just a moment,
to stop.

Try to take in all of the goodness
that you bestow upon my body
and to concentrate on
how lucky I am to have you in my life.
Because many people don't.
And I know that.
And yet

I forget.
And I take you for granted.
And I lust after pancakes
and sugar-laden lattes

and warm chocolate croissants
dipped in tea.

I'm sorry.
I'm a caterpillar.

It's not you, it's me.

— cm

Day 2: We were asked to write a poem about the process of traveling from one place to another.

Broken

It was a short drive to the funeral.
In the car, my mind focused on
a vision of your hand and
on the many journeys it had taken.
Your hand, with its broad fingers
and neatly trimmed nails,
palm worn with the wrinkles of time.
Your hand, so beautiful to me,
that cradled your beloved sons
long before I knew you,
that wore the same simple
wedding band for more than 50 years,
that snapped so many
stunning photographs,
captured some of the nation's
most turbulent times.
The hand that held a fishing rod
and threaded countless lines.
The hand that stitched the wounds
of a solider so well that it left no scar,
that always seemed to know
how to glue what was broken
back together again.
The hand that held your favorite tumbler
filled with Kentucky bourbon,
or that clapped whenever the Angels scored a run,
or that snapped apart your peanut brittle,
or that tossed jellybeans, three at a time,

into your upturned mouth.
The hand that, every May, placed American flags
beside the graves of those who had fallen,
that greeted beloved brothers,
and welcomed strangers,
and pulled close in an embrace all those you loved.
The hand that held your tiny granddaughter
on the day that she was born,
that tied her shoelaces,
that colored beside her,
that squeezed the oranges for her morning juice.
Your hand, so soft,
and damp with dying, that I held
as you slipped away from this life,
as you traveled from this finite frontier
into the eternal room next door.

— cm

Travel Directions

Don't look back.
One foot in front of the other.

Don't want to go.

Look both ways crossing streets.
Enjoy the scenery.

It's ugly.
Don't want to go.

Hands push.
Door slams.

Reluctant feet take first step.
Fist knuckles tears away.

Step, two, three, four
Step, two, three, four

— lh

Day 3: We were asked to write a poem inspired by an image of a Lythronax dinosaur skull fossil.

Trip to the Museum

The sign says this is a dinosaur,
Ly-thro-nax ar-ges-tes.
Anyone can see it's a dragon.
It probably *is* a gore king.
It flew here from somewhere
with huge leather wings and
guarded its treasure
in its mountain hideaway.

You can see where smoke
would come out of its nose
as it breathed fire. I expect
it could shoot fire a long way.
I bet I could find its treasure.

The boy rereads the museum plaque
then sprints off.

"Dad! Dad! Can we go camping
at Grand Staircase –
Es-co-lan-te National Monument
this weekend?"

— lh

Jest

Oh, Lythronax, you carnivore
  you king from our Southwest.
Oh, Lythronax, you loved your gore
  and didn't often jest.
Oh, Lythronax, such flesh you tore
  and with bone-crushing skill you were blessed.
Oh, Lythronax, I must confess
  I'm quite happy you are at rest.

— cm

Day 4: We were asked to write a poem about the literal or fig-
urative fabric of our lives.

Una Notte d'Estate

Your hand skims my shoulder
and my strap slips down my skin.
It tickles as it shimmies
and a fluttering begins
in my chest, at first,
and then settles in my shins.

The airy Indian cotton
feels cumbersome somehow.
Hot and heavy
a slight barrier to entry
It and I are having trouble
breathing now.

Skilled fingers sneak up my shirt
stop at the middle of my spine.
I wonder if you can feel
the sudden dampness of the fabric
and sense the headiness
I'm feeling from the wine.

Though, even in this state,
I begin to surmise
from your curious lips
and your toffee-colored eyes
that you like my matching bottoms
which makes me glad I got 'em

with their smooth penguin print
and their glorious hint
at a passel of possibilities
lying just beneath their surface
if only you could just get past the ties.
You could lay me down
on your fancy flannel sheets
and then be rewarded with my thighs,

which suddenly makes me nervous
and yet renews my sense of purpose.
And I'm reminded with a smile
that these pajamas were a present
from a caustic cousin
on a trip to London
who had a seriously impeccable sense of style.

She used to steal my cashmere socks
to stuff her bra — her only flaw —
and as you draw my shirt up over my head
discarding my finely blended threads
I remember when she handed me the gift
she said, "Good luck getting laid
wearing those."

— cm

Fabric of My Life

My mother, a fabric maven,
taught me to love it too.
In the store bolts and bolts
of cloth stood upright on shelves.
Usually classed together by type,
then by color, mother could
imagine how it would look
turned into an outfit. I could
only say if I liked it or not.

She loved fabric, the richer
the feel, color, pattern, the better.
When she died, I found drawers
filled with gorgeous fabric.
I took it home to add to my own collection.
Sometimes I pulled out a piece to make something.
Mostly I admired it, fingered it
with happy fingers, and said – one day...
That day never arrived.

When I moved across the country
the fabric had to go. I gathered
my sewing friends together:
"Help yourself." I hope they make
beautiful items out of it
not just store it away as we did.
All those yards of fabulous fabric
want to be made into something spectacular.

—lh

Day 5: A link was provided which, when clicked on, took the participant to a random Wikipedia article, the subject of which would be the subject of the day's poem. The poem could be informative or not, according to the participant's inclinations. "Mameluke Sword" came up for Lynn, "St. Louis Blues" for Chloé.

The Mameluke Sword

It hung over the mantlepiece
in horizontal splendor.
The boy wondered if an ancestor
had killed anyone with it.
Would there be blood on
the blade? Encased in its scabbard,
he couldn't see the blade.
Did it cut on both edges?
If only one, which one?
He would practice imagining
the sharp edge on the inside curve
like the scythe his grandfather
used in the meadow.
Every time he swung the imagined sword
in front of him, he feared cutting himself.
He decided the sharp edge had to be
the outside curve. He knew one day
he would be strong enough
to lift it down, take it out of its scabbard.
Then – off with their heads.
He couldn't wait.

— lh

Handy

Fine fingers float
across dancing wooden keys
racing and romping
gamboling and grooving
brushes swirling across
drums and metal
and a striking siren
sings a song of longing
while maintaining
a splash of sass
in her sway

— cm

Day 6: We were asked to write a poem about the feeling of time passing and its effect on you.

Fade

These days, I stare in the mirror
and take in the big bunch of white hairs
that have begun to line the right side of my face
the side with a cheek bone
that used to sit higher
used to look tighter.

All at once, it seems,
they've arrived.

At my birthday party
a girl of six sat with me
as I blew out the candles on my cake.

"How olllllddd are you?" she asked me.
"I'm 41," I said.
"41!" she moaned and then declared
"Well, I'm not old!
I'm young!"
And she hopped off my lap and
sprinted away.

Disappeared before I knew
where she had run off to.
Slipped into nothing,
as youth will do.

— cm

End in Sight

I never doubted one day
I would cease to be –
just not yet.

When the doctor gave
the irrefutable diagnosis that death approached
I had to shift gears.

With a finite amount of time available,
I don't squander it
bemoaning the past, fearing the future.

Now is what I have –
each moment precious,
each breath a miracle.

— lh

Day 7: We were asked to write a poem inspired by an image of assorted seeds, grains, and clusters of dried leaves, which were sorted into small piles and resting on a wooden surface.

Switching Roles

The artist spent all afternoon
arranging seeds and plant material
on the smooth table making its grain
intrinsic to the design. She knew
the Billy Balls, of course,
recognized corn and pumpkin seeds.
The tiny lavender seeds
held a hint of scent, more astringent than sweet,
reminding her of the handmade sachets
in her Christmas stocking.
She stepped back to cast a critical eye
on the still life. After several adjustments
she left to fetch her camera.
She always took a photo before she painted.

As she returned to her studio,
the outside door flew open.
Her son and a gust of wind charged in.
The still life few in all directions,
an afternoon's work lost.
"Aren't you glad to see me, Mom?"
She gathered him in.
She would clean up later.

— lh

Heirloom

Because of you,
I understand that
in the seed rests
not only flavor
and bounty
but also forgotten cultures,
family histories,
a unique connection
to our future and our past.
You protectors of the pollinators,
you guardians of extinct
and resurrected cuisines,
you stewards of
ancient knowledge,
and abundant diversity,
thank you for teaching me
about these treasured sources
and precious gifts of life.
You are full-hearted
healers of the earth.

— cm

Day 8: We were asked to write a poem where every line started with "I am" or "I think".

Maureen Maunders

I am often late for hair appointments and
I am not sure why and
I am ashamed to admit this but
I am also someone who laughs at funerals because
I am uncomfortable with grief and death. And
I am sorry that
I am not a better adult at this point in my life but
I am doing the best I can.
I am learning about how to eat more whole grains and
I am cutting out sugar and
I am trying to meditate for fifteen minutes in the morning
    when
I am just getting started with my day but
I am still stressed out all of the time and, to be honest,
I am not sure I can stay sober for another entire month because
I am a serious addict and
I am surfing on a friend's couch at the moment and
I am allergic to her cats and her bird and
I am feeling claustrophobic and like
I am clawing at the walls to make my escape.
I am grateful for the place to crash of course and
I am working on getting a part-time job so that
I am able to afford my cell phone so my parents can stop
    reminding me that
I am too old to support and that I need to get a life and grow up
    already because
I am placing them in an uncomfortable position as they feel
    concerned that

I am "going to wind up dead in a dumpster" and
I am keeping them up at night and making my mom's anxiety
  worse.
I am not sure I believe that, frankly, because my mother has
  always been high-strung and
I am not the only cause of her misery and her perpetual
  disenchantment with life.
I am tired of being blamed just because I find existence hard
  and because
I am struggling to not get high and I don't know how to do that
  well. At least
I am trying. At least
I am trying. At least
I am friggin' trying, right? Mostly I have to remind myself that
  even though
I am often obsessive and pretty emotional and usually sad as
  hell, even though
I am not perfect,
I am still enough, and
I am someone who is worthy of love, just because
I am.

— cm

Alexander's Breastplate

I am mad
I am sad
I am bad
I am glad

I am green
I am mean
I am keen
I am seen

I am late
I am fate
I am bait
I am great

I am never blander
I am getting grander
I am a grandstander
I am Alexander

— lh

Day 9: We were asked to write a poem that unfolds this story:
"They washed up on the beach at dusk..."

Patience Rewarded

Alexander paced up and down the beach.
His dream told him they would come.
He trusted his dreams. They'd never been wrong.
Not once.

The sun was high in the sky.
Alexander still walked back and forth.
His mother brought him a peanut butter
and jelly sandwich and a thermos of milk.
She put a blanket on a large rock.
Alexander grinned and
sat down on it to eat his lunch.
As the air grew cooler, he wrapped
the blanket around himself still waiting.

They washed up on the beach at dusk.
Alexander hurried over to help
the tiny sailors off the schooner.
He watched them fade away
into the grass on the hill.
Only the captain remained.
He never left his ship.
Tucking the ship under his arm,
Alexander hurried home.

"You found your boat," his dad said,
His mother dished up hot stew
in the large bowls on the table.
He heard her reciting poetry as she worked.

Home is the sailor, home from the sea,
*And the hunter home from the hill.**

Alexander gave her a bear hug.
"Wash up for supper," she said.

He hurried off to the pump.
"You can show me what's in the hold later,"
he whispered to the captain. The captain
saluted smartly before retiring to his cabin.

— lh

from "Requiem" by Robert Louis Stevenson

Bouquet

There they were —
two rough lumps of rare ambergris
wallowing in the waters off the coast of Morecambe Bay.
A pair of sopping, crusty candles to the touch.
A whiteish bit of not-quite-feces from a species
of sperm whale,
which will earn a pretty penny and be used
to make perfume.

— cm

Day 10: We were asked to write a mirror/palindrome poem.

Secluded

No one seems to find me here
I exist within an emptiness
Always teetering on the brink of blackness
Despair
I peer into my shadows and discover
Again and again
I am no one I know

I am no one I know
Again and again
I peer into my shadows and discover
Despair
Always teetering on the brink of blackness
I exist within an emptiness
No one seems to find me here

— cm

turn about

birds fly
hens screech
herds flock
preachers preach

frogs leap
donkeys bray
dogs howl
children play

play children
howl dogs
bray donkeys
leap frogs

preach preachers
flock herds
screech hens
fly birds.

about turn

— lh

Day 11: We were asked to look inside the nearest trash can and write a poem about what we found there.

Profiler at Work

Alexander looks at the trash
surrounding him on the floor.

<u>Meticulous</u> (his favorite new word this week) –
    all recyclables are clean – cans/jars –
    broken down, neatly folded – cardboard boxes;
<u>Female</u> – catalogues of fancy stuff like jewelry;
<u>Artist</u> – catalogues of art supplies;
<u>Not a Cook</u> – instant oatmeal box, bullion cube jar,
    empty Weight Watcher meal containers;
<u>Concerned about Weight</u> – see above;
    (Why?)
<u>Cares for Environment</u> – cuts plastic can loops apart;
    recycles everything;
<u>Keeps Name Private not Address</u> – mail has name and address
    torn out unless to resident;
<u>Tea Drinker</u> – folded empty teabag boxes;
<u>Addicted to Chocolate and Peanut Butter</u> – multiple large
    boxes of chocolate in different forms;
    huge empty peanut butter jars;
<u>May Be Spy</u> – shredder hidden under desk; nothing personal
    in trash

More information needed.
Alexander signs his report.

— lh

Vulgar

In the bathroom trash,
a used Q-tip from this morning,
yellow tint at one end.
Maybe that swift swipe of my ear
will finally help me to listen better
pay closer attention to
the people I love.

Used pads,
bloodied
and wrapped in toilet tissue,
as if there is a need to cover
up my crimson secret,
to hide the truth, even from me.
I bleed
but soon all of that will stop.
How many years before
that machinery grinds
to a final halt?

And then,
how many more years before
pads become pampers
and blood becomes urine
and I will no longer be able to hear
a song
or a scream
or a sigh?

— cm

Day 12: We were asked to write a poem about a smell that floods our memory every time we smell it.

Familiar

The first blooms of summer
a sea of yellow roses
sway just outside the
screened-in porch

Hints of fruits and clove
like a perfume of pretending
and for a few perfect seconds
I breathe in deeply, and

forget that you once brought me
a bouquet for my birthday
and now you no longer know me
when I call your name

— cm

Orange Peels

Every day we served two lunches:
one to the morning children,
the other to the afternoon class –
lunches for thirty starving
four-year-olds. Each lunch had
a sandwich, a small carton of milk
and a large round orange.

No one in the kitchen scored
the oranges. No knives or
sharp scissors were allowed
in the classroom. Four-year-old fingers
cannot peel the tough rind.
Day after day, month after month,
we broke open 30 oranges
with our fingernails.

For nine months I could not get
the smell of orange peel
out from under my fingernails.
I learned to hate a smell
I once savored. Even now,
half a century later,
peeling an orange makes me gag.

— lh

Day 13: We were asked to write a poem about the weather outside at that moment.

Weather Report

April 13, 2019, 10:23 A.M.
South Mountain, Salt Lake County
Temperature 43^0
Sun breaking through clouds
melting light snow.
After days of cold, wet weather
bringing large amounts of snow
at higher elevations,
we expect a warmer, drier trend
for today. Our newly greening trees
show little wind movement at ground level.

Some blue sky over midsection
of valley. Salt Lake City
and Antelope Island still hidden
behind a solid grey bank of slow-moving clouds.
White clouds over central area inch across the valley
toward Wasatch mountains. May dump
more snow there. Peaks of the mountain ranges
to the east and west are still hidden
beneath low angry clouds.

Enjoy the sun. More rain will be arriving
by late afternoon into tomorrow.
Utah's daffodils, forsythia, pear and cherry trees
continue to put forth their spring colors
undefeated by winter's reluctance to
vacate our slopes – true harbingers of spring.   — lh

Tu-a-wee

Bright spring sun
   in a cloudless azure sky
Bluebirds sing to one another
   of the heat
   and the beauty

— cm

Day 14: We were asked to write a poem inspired by an image of a beaded Ute cradle board, which was made in the mid-to-late 1900s.

Ghosts

The cradleboard is not yellow, but
I still wonder if you were a girl.
I wonder about the soft white fabric
and how your grandmother gathered
and laced the brain-tanned buckskin
tightly around your innocent body,
praying for your safety.

I think about her skilled fingers
stitching the intricate beadwork with love
patterns of blue, red, orange and green.
A bit of added beauty to celebrate your birth.
I wonder if your grandmother was a warrior
and whether she was haunted by ghosts.

I wonder about our ancestors
and all we learn and inherit from them
about historic trauma
and the burdens we are born into.
I wonder about protective sunshades
made of twined willow
and about all they cannot hope to protect.

— cm

Lullaby for a Ute Baby

Hush, Little One, Mama's here.
Hush, Little One, Papa's near.
Close your sleepy little eyes.
When you wake – a big surprise.
Sleep.
Sleep.
Sleep.

Look, Little One, Mama made
cradle with a willow shade.
It will hold you all day long,
while I sing you cradle song.
Sleep.
Sleep.
Sleep.

— lh

Day 15: We were asked to write a haiku only using words from a piece of junk mail or an advertisement.

water reflections
positive and negative
painting wet landscapes

— lh

come festive summer
with your beach time and sunshine
your beauty is free

— cm

Day 16: We were asked to write a poem from the point of view of a fire.

Beware the Salesman

Summers in Southern California
are simply divine.
I couldn't ask for better surroundings.
So many opportunities for growth
and the weather is pretty perfect —
dry heat and a pleasant breeze,
lots of dense forests, tall grasses, and such.
And you know I can't stand the rain.
It puts such a damper on things.

Plus, I'm really popular with the locals,
especially the smokers and the hikers.
Seems like the majority of the time
they're eager to make friends
and really ignite my spark
so to speak.
It's amazing how when I
meet the right person
at just the right time
I feel suddenly set ablaze
with a sense of freedom and ambition.

Some people are afraid of me.
They see me as unrelenting
and a bit destructive,
but I feel like I've got a pretty
warm personality, overall.
I'm super dynamic

I keep things interesting
and I'm always on the move.
I mean, at least until I run out of energy.
I know I can be a bit too intense sometimes
and that can cause some damage
but all I really need is a long, cold shower
and then I calm right down.

I'm really not that intimidating at all.
If I had a dating profile, it might read:
Wild and flashy
with a love of fresh air
large open spaces
and the wind at my back.
Enjoys pushing boundaries
flirting late at night
and staying smoking hot.
If you can just figure out how
to tame my blazing spirit
you'll be charmed by my luminosity,
and my all-consuming nature
won't seem nearly as scary.
You'll want to snuggle up close
and drift off to sleep.

— cm

Fire Asks Questions

Why do I get a bad rap?
I bear no malice towards
anyone or anything.
My destiny is to burn.
That's what I was created for.

Why am I blamed?
I do not self-ignite.
Something has to bring me alive.
The spark comes from outside of me.
Why do people forget that?

Why do you think I get out of control?
I'm like wind and water.
I go where I must. Wind blows me.
Water squelches me.
None of this is my choice.

Why don't you keep me
in a proper container
where I can gift light and heat?
I'm always hungry, need to be fed.
It's my nature.

Don't scream at me about
forests, witches, cathedrals.
I'm continuously starved
but not intentionally destructive.
Why don't you understand?

I'm beautiful and useful
when harnessed. I'm willing to work
with you. Stop blaming me for things
not my fault. Can't we work together?
You need me more than I need you.

— lh

Day 17: We were asked to write an epitaph for an inanimate object.

Anthea, Robert, Cyril, Jane, and Lamb

Five verdigris children
played in gardens, until movers
smashed their bodies
in horror trip from East to West,
now landfill denizens.
Rest in peace.

— lh

May the Workhorse Rest in Peace

Here lies our Sweet Silver Fox Mac-cine,
who died when a drunk neighbor punched her screen.
For years, she remained sharp and virus-free.
So much for thinking differently.

— cm

Day 18: We were asked to write a poem about our favorite urban legend, piece of folklore, or fairy tale.

Flood

100 years later
   down by the waterfront
some people swear
   they can still smell
   the sweet aroma
   of molasses
wafting through the
   stifling August air

— cm

Just the Facts Ma'am

The memoir is coming along.
Don't know how to handle
my grandfather's fairy tale
that is now an entrenched
legend believed by everyone.

He was something of a trickster,
my grandfather. We knew some
of his stories were exactly that,
not to be taken as fact.
Popwolliger's Island
doesn't exist, nor does
Maggie Snipe. She lived
in the gutter and was gifted
with terrible habits not to be copied.

Some of us knew Gramps
had a difficult childhood.
It was easy to believe he ran away
from home at age eight.
The way he told it, many still believe
he worked as a water boy
during the construction
of the Brooklyn Bridge.

I love the Brooklyn Bridge.
One day, walking across it,
I read a plaque.
Scales fell from my eyes.
The Brooklyn Bridge was completed

in 1883. Gramps was born in 1885.
Do I tell the facts or let the legend live on?

— lh

Day 19: We were asked to write a poem about forgetting something important.

How Could I Have Forgotten?

Good Friday is a solemn day
for Christians worldwide –
different from the first one.
We know Easter is coming.
They had no idea.

At the Stations of the Cross service,
a lay reader reads part of each station.
I am often the reader for the noon service.
The one requirement is to stay detached.

Once I forget to keep
my emotional armor on.
At the thirteenth station
I might as well have been
in Jerusalem with Mary.
The dead body of her son
is placed in her lap.
By the time I arrive at the last words –
"call me Mara (which means Bitter);
for the Lord has dealt bitterly with me,"
tears pour down my cheeks.
Sobs choke my voice.
Somehow, I manage to regain control
for the last station.

I am never again asked to read on Good Friday.   — lh

Seize

Stubby fingers shove
themselves inside of my shorts.

As they do this,
I lose count of how many times
I told him No.

Or of how many times I pushed
his malevolent mouth away from
my body.

I forget, in that moment,
that my body belongs to me.
I forget that I have a body.
I forget what it feels like,
to be safe
and to be free.

— cm

Day 20: We were asked to write a poem inspired by an image of two beekeepers wearing their white beekeeping gear while harvesting honey.

Clarity

I wish I could have seen clearly
through your smoke and disguises.
You always seemed to be
confusing my defenses
numbing my senses
silencing all the alarms
so you could take what you wanted
raid what little I had saved for myself.

You were never concerned with my survival
or with how hard I'd worked to get here,
only about your quick reward
your insatiable appetite for what comes easily.
You'd call me Queen, while clipping my wings.
You'd say you can't live without me, while stealing
all of the hard-earned nectar of my life
from right underneath my nose.

You really are just like the bear, the skunk,
the clever predator who smashes and grabs
and your white robes won't fool me anymore.

— cm

The Aliens Have Landed

Alexander and his dad walked
with the new puppy through the fields.
Sometimes the boy ran ahead,
then returned to his dad who was holding the leash.
"Can he run with me, Dad?"
"Not yet, son. He's too young."
"But I want him to."
"One day, when he's properly trained."

The boy ran ahead again. He arrived
at a hedge, peeked through.
What he saw prevented another step,
almost stopped his breathing.
He ran back to his father. "Dad, Dad,
we need to turn around
and go straight back home."
"Why, Alexander?"
"The aliens have landed right over
that hedge." He pointed with shaking hand.

"Nonsense," said his dad.
"I'm telling you. I saw them. Let's get out of here."
His dad took Alexander by the hand and walked
toward the hedge. Alexander pulled back hard.
"Stop it, Alexander." As he turned to get a firmer grip
on his son's wrist, the puppy pulled loose and dove through the
hedge.

Alexander shouted, "No!" He plowed through the hedge
after his puppy. The shouts made the aliens turn around.

One scooped the puppy up and headed toward the boy
and his father. "Not a good place for a little guy," he said.
"You don't want him stung." Then he turned back to his work.

"See," hissed Alexander. His dad tried not to laugh.
"They're not aliens, son.
They're beekeepers harvesting honey.
You're quite right, though. It is time to head for home."

— lh

Day 21: We were asked to write a poem about a favorite picture book we read when we were younger.

Library Treat

At the library I would grab
Johnny Crow's Garden
off the low shelf before looking
at any other book. Written in 1903
by L. Leslie Brooke, its illustrations
were a combination
of pen and ink line drawings
and watercolor paintings.
The animals were characters with feelings.
I loved the words most.
It rhymed, easy to memorize.
The vocabulary assumed intelligence.
The sound was elegant. I reveled in it.
"While the Elephant
    Said something quite irrelevant."
I hated every child who took out *my* book.

— lh

Aplomb

A little blue engine
   climbs a steep hill
puffing along
   practicing courage

— cm

Day 22: We were asked to write an Ode to a produce item.

To Smell You Is to Know You

Oh, Arugula, you bitter, bitter green
So much more complex than you initially seem
You are fresh, peppery, and good for me, too
I'm so honored to create this ode to you.
Oh, Arugula, you garden rocket divine
I think of you with appreciation whenever I dine.
You wild aphrodisiac of Ancient Rome
Banned until Charlemagne said we could grow you at home.
Oh, Arugula, you put other greens to the test.
And, all things considered, I love thee the best.

Oh, Arugula, better than spinach you taste
And you're now grown commercially all over the place.
Some like you on pizza, in soup, or with fish
But however we use you, you are always delish.
Oh, Arugula, certain moth larvae like you, too
At 90 percent water, you're the perfect hydrating food
You've got antioxidants, and fiber, and Vitamin K
And you're rich in glucosinolates, which help keep cancer
    away.
Oh, Arugula, you always want for my greatest good
And I plan to eat more of you, for I know that I should.

Oh, Arugula, you're so nutrient dense
Learning to love you is just common sense.
You pack such a powerful nutritional punch
And I can enjoy you at breakfast, dinner, or lunch.
Oh, Arugula, I'm glad you're buddies with Swiss Chard and
    Kale

I'll be buying you together again when you go on sale.
And in the meantime, Arugula, please remain pure
Keep organic when you can, that way you'll be sure.
Oh, Arugula, my dear Eruca, I just want you to know
That the world got such a gift the day that you began to grow.

— cm

Ode to the Tomato

Dear tomāto, tomăto – however you say it,
its flavor superb, its shape so comely.
Whatever the cost I am willing to pay it
because there has never been any too homely
to garnish a salad, brighten the taste,
embrace the pasta, meld all the stew,
layered in sandwich, or fresh from the vine.
All of you edible so there's no waste.
For so many dishes you are the glue
that holds food together like heady wine.

Pity the poor person allergic to you.
However you're used you enhance the flavor.
If they can't eat tomatoes, they'd have no clue,
without your ingredient nothing to savor.
How bland every meal, no beautiful red,
no more spaghetti to twirl on their spoon.
Grilled cheese without your soup? I'd weep.
The food on a plate would look totally dead –
No charming tomato? I'd softly croon,
"What's the use of eating? Might as well sleep."

Never to know a cherry tomato
or relish lasagna layer on layer?
Almost as bad as no sweet potato –
definitely becomes wicked taste slayer.
Surely tomatoes were a gift from the gods
meant to be loved and cherished the most.
I pity the people who have to say no.
Imagine a meal without it, poor sods.

Oh, tomato, I raise up my glass and give toast:
To the gorgeous tomato that thrills my heart so.

— lh

Day 23: We were asked to write a poem about when we felt least understood.

What Happened?

I chose my college for its writing major,
dropped the year I arrived. A voracious reader,
lit became my major.

My senior year my faculty advisor
said the department didn't know
what to do with me.
The Freudian-centered professors
didn't like my papers, admittedly dreadful.
I didn't know how to feed them
what they wanted. We didn't speak
the same language.

My advisor suggested switching
to education, one of the few times
I ever blew up at authority.
"You should encourage your best students
to go into education, not your worst.
What do you think I would want to teach?"
Shocked, he raised his shoulders
in that I don't know way.
"Lit, of course," I thundered.
The horror on his face was laughable.

All seniors were required to take
The lit AGRE* exam to graduate.
I scored so high, they had to give me an A.
I'd done the work, understood, in my way,

60

the readings. No one believed my score.
I'm sure he would be horrified
if he found out I did teach
English and American Literature.
Honestly, I was good.

— lh

*Advanced Graduate Record Exam

Imperfect

He's so handsome
she says to me.
Yes, but he has a temper.
Oh, all men have tempers,
she responds with a laugh.
They can't all
be perfect, you know.

— cm

Day 24: We were asked to write a tricube poem. In a tricube, each line contains 3 syllables; each stanza contains 3 lines; and each poem contains 3 stanzas.

Nocturnal

Suddenly
the rain fell
and I slept

I dreamed then
of vast fields
fireflies

your gray eyes
and dancing
in the dark

— cm

Prognosis

Doctor said
terminal
Mind went blank

Oxygen
delivered
ten p. m.

Was surprised
to wake up
next morning

— lh

Day 25: We were asked to write a poem about a current or former home.

126 Adelphi Street

I did not fall in love when I first saw it.
I hated it, feared it.
My gut screamed,
"NO!"
Six weeks later we moved in.

It came with two tenants:
a family of four squeezed into four small rooms
on the third floor, one woman on the top floor.
Everyone said, "Never buy a place with tenants."

Our part had two full kitchens,
a bath and a half, no proper bedrooms,
roaches, and mice. Parents and two boys
moved in with a very pregnant Siamese,
and her mate – a week later, three newborn kittens.
The cats took care of the mice.

Saving grace was the backyard with
four saucer magnolias and a mulberry tree –
a safe place for the boys to play.
The rickety fence didn't keep burglars out.
They also came down the coal hatch and
up the fire escape. We put in alarms,
built a new fence.

We tore down a tacky roof over the patio.
Mistake. When it rained, the drain filled

with mulberries and magnolia petals in the spring,
leaves in the fall. The house flooded. All night
someone had to run out in bare feet to clear
the drain. Of course, that someone was often me.

It was a disaster house in so many ways,
yet I learned to love it. I cried when we bought it,
sobbed harder when we sold it and moved on.

— lh

Maturation

I thought I'd grow old
in that backyard
surrounded by the
lush greenness
your gaudy statuary
and the weeping
cherry tree
we planted together
when it was just
a sapling.

Even though
that rickety wooden swing
was on its last legs back then,
I still somehow imagined
I'd be swinging on it
until I died.

Whenever I close my eyes
I am transported there.
I see the fieldstone wall
that dear Tatù built
and the neighbors' kids
tramping across it
which always drove you insane.

I see the pink and purple
azalea bushes
and the hostas surrounding

the uneven steps that led to
the magical fairyland I loved.

I used to imagine that
that no one could see me
back there, at home
with the silence
and the bunnies
and the bees.

But now I know better
and boy how things change
and the weeping cherry tree is
no longer a baby
and the swing has collapsed now
and the neighbors' kids
have all gone off to college
and they don't give a damn
about your volatility or your rage.

No, you are alone now,
alone with your statues
and all the walls you've erected
and not even your daffodils
can lie for you anymore.

— cm

Day 26: We were asked to write a poem inspired by two paintings of sandpipers featured in a first edition copy of John James
Audubon's *The Birds of America*. In each of the paintings, one
bird is dipping its beak into the water, while the other looks off
into the distance.

Discontent

Our sensitive bills
probe for food
seek out the usual suspects,
insects,
crustaceans,
maybe a worm or two.
Frankly, I'm exhausted from
our non-stop flights
which are getting to be so tedious

and our elaborate
courtship displays
which almost always
end predictably
with the same
shallow depression of
a nest,
leaves, moss,
the same old, same old.

And then the usual four
blotchy-brown eggs,
no surprises there.
And once they've hatched

then does he stay?
Or does she stay?
And so the dance begins.

And I like our friends all right
but it just seems like we're always together.
You know the saying,
birds of a feather...
I just need a little space.

This afternoon,
I picked my head up from the sand
glanced off at the water,
and started dreaming of a different life
of a deeper sense of purpose.

For a moment, I actually fantasized about being
a budgie, one of those beloved
pet parakeets that can snuggle and talk.
I imagined that maybe John James Audubon
himself would come and catch sight of us
in our natural habitat
and think us interesting enough to
capture in one of his original drawings
maybe we'd even make it into one of his books.
Maybe we'd wind up celebrities, Sandy and me.

Maybe I could get my sensitive bill
altered a bit, just a few inches shorter,
nothing crazy.
Maybe some different colors,
something a bit more like one of those
scarlet-banded barbets we've seen
down in South America...
Who knows?

I think it'd be really wild, though,
to think that our mundane existences
would actually count for something
that someone might find a simple sketch of us
many years in the future
and say, "Wow, look at those beautiful birds.
How amazing they must have been!"

They would gather around
and they'd marvel.
How wonderful that would be,
to be appreciated
to matter
to live on.

— cm

John James Audubon's Birds

Did you know some brilliant person
convinced the library in 1903
to purchase a secondhand original copy
of the 1860 John James Audubon's
The Birds of America folio?
It cost $230, a huge amount then.

Now in a glass case on the fourth floor,
it takes four librarians to turn
one 27" x 40" double elephant sheet
to a new painting. It wasn't put under glass
until 1972. Before that library patrons,
including children, could actually handle
this treasure. The results of the wear and tear
are clearly visible on the title page.

On the current open page sandpipers are
on the beach, in the marshes.
Their long, slender bills poke for food or water.
One can almost see them scuttling along,
their thin black legs moving rapidly.

The semipalmated sandpipers
have partially webbed toes.
They nest in the arctic tundra.
How did Audubon know that?

The male curlew sandpiper has
rusty-red breeding plumage,
is a vagrant in America.

The curlew breeds in the arctic Siberian tundra
and winters from southern Australia to South Africa.
Any curlew in America must have been
blown way off course. Audubon mentions
how rare they are here. How did he know?
Unfortunately, he's not here to ask.
I wish he were.

— lh

Day 27: We were asked to write a poem about the town of
Shoyna, Russia.

The Inexorable Sand

Shoyna, Russia, is a desert
on the Kanin Peninsula by the White Sea.
Not an ancient place, the village sprang up in the thirties
to house fishermen and their families.
Where once inhabitants had a collective farm,
including small plots by the houses and meadows for cows,
all is now shifting sand.

The fleet of seventy fishing boats
sailed in and out of the harbor emptying the sea
of its fish while trawlers scraped the bottom clean
of seaweed and silt. The fishery closed down
when the catch dried up. The brickyard is gone.
The land once farmed is now arid, dune covered.
The sea churns the untethered sand onto the shore.
The wind blows it over Shoyna.
A house can be obliterated in one night.

A bulldozer pushes the sand away.
The wind hurls it back. Doors are
left open so one can get out. First
floors fill with sand. Windows are
often covered midway up the second
story. The sand makes a scratchy sound
on the glass and stings faces.
Children play and slide on the dunes
while adults shovel sand day after day.

74

The once bustling village is almost a ghost town.
A diesel plant provides electricity
but there's no sewage disposal or running water.
Water is dipped out of wells. Women bathe
Tuesdays and Wednesdays in the bathhouse,
men Thursdays and Fridays. They order bread ahead
because the bakery is only open four days.
Most supplies come by ship. The only other way
to reach Shoyna is by small plane or helicopter
that lands on a short, sand covered runway.

People stay because they say they are free there.
Sand continues to bury them.
Someday the red and white striped
decommissioned lighthouse, 105 feet tall,
may be the one remaining landmark
to show anyone ever lived there.

— lh

Sand Stories

This is not a place
for stilettos.
Legs grow weary
too quickly here.
Backs break from
hard work
and harvesting mushrooms.
Old villagers reminisce
about grassy fields,
neighbors' farms,
and heroic fishermen.
But those days are long gone now.

You can still find fish —
white salmon, sole, haddock, navaga,
but nothing like when
dozens of ships
were coming in every day
crowding the quay.
A few abandoned vessels still
dot the shoreline
proof that life here was
once different.
Now those rusting shadows
of their former greatness
shield battered houses
from crashing waves.

In the summers,
small planes fly overhead,

sometimes
landing on the dirt path runway.
Men on large boats deliver supplies.
Researchers come
to study the birds.
Reindeer herders
visit from time to time
and trade meat
for Arctic cloudberries
from the tundra.

In the frigid winters,
the river freezes over
and the houses are heated with firewood
found buried on the beach.
There are dog sleds and snowmobiles
and shovels to share
and dancing on Saturday nights.
Sometimes the local soldiers come.

And then there is the wind,
the violent westerly wind that whips along
the coast of the White Sea
bringing with it
the unrelenting sand
the ghosts of the benthos.

It blows in past
the striped lighthouse and shakes
the weather-beaten windows while they sleep,
after praying they will not be entombed overnight
trusting that they will still
be able to crawl out the front doors they
always leave open
or some hole they've cut into the attic

to get down to the bathhouse
on Tuesdays, if you're a girl.

Bulldozing is in high demand here
and birth rates spike
when the power goes out.
Sand blocks the sunlight from
streaming into living rooms
where tea is drunk with water
drawn from the well.

It seems they are always
digging out of some dune
or other hollow.
The jobs are scarce
but the geese and
the seagull eggs
are plentiful.

This is home.
A secluded sandbox.
A slice of serenity.
A seabed that remembers.
And lately,
spots of grass,
growing again.

— cm

Day 28: We were asked to write a poem inspired by an image of a bison-hide moccasin, dated AD 1225-1275, which was discovered in Promontory Cave I in Box Elder County, Utah in the 1930s.

Vision

Little sole
Still smelling of smoke
Leather worn at the heel
Imprint of a child's foot
Kept warm in harsh winters

Little soul
Once danced beside flames
Mother fed you bison
She laughed and sang you songs
And kissed your chilly toes

— cm

A Small Moccasin

The boy looks at everything
in the Indian exhibit. He stops in front of
a small moccasin. He stares at it
a long time. He says to his mother,
 "I think it might fit my foot."
She nods. "Then the Indian who wore it,
could be a boy just like me."
"Possibly."
"I'd like to play cowboys and Indians
with him. Can I ask him, Mom? Can I?"

She sighs. "Alexander, I'm sure
he would love to play with you, but
it will have to be pretend play.
He lived a long time ago.
He'll be all grown up now."
Alexander thinks a few minutes.
"Jim and I want to play outside
and then get ice cream." His mother
takes his hand as they walk back
to the elevator. "If he gets too tired
you may have to help him eat his ice cream."
"Don't let the door close on Jim."

The mother holds the door open.
She understands.

— lh

Day 29: We were asked to write a poem about something that
has a terrible texture.

Terrible Texture

Don't speak to me about textured
walls. Besides hurting my skin,
they collect dust, grease,
little boys' jelly fingerprints,
and are impossible to clean.

Why would anyone use paint
with sand or worse in it? Why
wallpaper over it? Have you scraped
wallpaper off a bumpy wall?

Worst job ever. You never get it all.
A sander makes no headway.
Sponges quickly rip to shreds.
My hands were a bloody mess.
Should have put up sheetrock.

Painting? Because the surface
is rough you must use
a deep napped roller,
heavy, filled with paint.
You roll in every direction,
still find holidays.*

Did I mention the wall over the stairwell?
That's where the roller falls off the broom handle
and bounces down the stairs. Thump. Splat.

Thump. Splat. Thump. Splat.
To the bottom. Three times.
As I said, do not speak to me
about textured walls.

— lh

holidays – spots missed by the painter

Bad Fad

A disturbing memory of
a distant dinner party
and a pretty pink platter
lined with layers of lettuce
and like a neophobe's nightmare
frozen in time,
a lemon-flavored
jelly "salad ring"
fresh out of the 60s
and bursting
with vinegar-soaked
cabbage, thin slivers of radish,
and slices of hard-boiled eggs
suspended and seeming
to shiver with every step
I took in their jiggling,
gelatinous direction.

My mind will never
forget that image
nor the mouthfeel
of the slippery
minced chives.

— cm

Day 30: We were asked to write a poem about an ending.

Peace

I said to Shame,
I think it's time
to seriously rethink
our relationship.

I said,
You've held me back
and you've hurt me
and you've told me
so many lies.

For far too long,
I've given you power
you didn't deserve to have.
I've believed you
and I've dreamed small
dreams because of it.

I said,
You've encouraged
and enabled me
to betray myself and
to abandon myself
over and over again.

I said to Shame,
I understand now
that you're not okay.

But the thing is, I am.
And after today,
I've finally decided
you aren't welcome here
anymore.

— cm

Last of Her Generation

for Jim

We gather together
from our scattered homes
for our grandmother's funeral.
She lived her last years in Maine
with our aunt, who brings her back home
to upstate New York to be buried
next to her husband
and the son who died too young.
We feel grateful to be reunited.
She was the glue who kept us
connected with her loving letters
as she once gathered us together
for every holiday dinner.

We go out to eat at our favorite restaurant
during the break between visiting hours.
I look around the table and voice
what we all are feeling. "She is loving
us sitting here eating together, all dressed up,
enjoying each other's company."
I hope she hears my cousin's comment.
"And not a lemon in the bunch."

— lh

A Conversation
with the Poets

Who Are Writers?

CM: If you're reading this and you think that you are a writer, my guess is that you probably are. You might not yet be a *professional* writer or an *experienced* writer, but you are probably a writer. You probably have the "soul" of a writer.

I believe there are folks out there who are just *aching* to write their stories and for whatever reason they haven't yet been able to begin. Maybe they have begun and then stopped for long periods of time for one reason or another. Maybe writing seems impossible while raising a family. Maybe chronic illness blocks the energy to write. Maybe it's actually dangerous to write about certain topics. Maybe one simply isn't quite sure about story structure and that holds one back from writing. I still believe those people are writers. They just aren't writing at the moment. Hopefully that will change. I don't believe we have to be published to be a writer. I don't think we have to be making money at our craft to be a writer. I don't even think we need to share our work with others to be a writer, although I wonder if we aren't losing something special by not ever experiencing a reader's reactions to our work.

Sometimes we create stories in our hearts for a really long time before words spill out onto a page. Sometimes, when the words don't come easily, or they don't come for a long time, or we've been too scared to even try to write, we think, I'm not *really* a writer. I'm not *really* a writer unless I have a book deal. I'm not *really* a writer unless I'm writing every single day." At some point, writers actually do need to write. But even before that, I believe that if we know in our heart that we're a writer and we can claim that for ourselves, then that's a vital thing to be able to do. We have to believe in ourselves as writers, even when no one else believes in us yet. That seed of self-belief can give us the confidence to actually begin.

LH: One of the reasons we dared to put this book together is because we want people to see that not everything one writes is perfect. A lot of it isn't. We want people to understand, as in any profession, one has to learn one's craft. We write many words. Some of them don't work. My poems that are really terrible, strike me funny. The ones that are mediocre are the ones that break my heart, because somehow or another I have a hard time making them into anything other than mediocre. I do know that the more I write, the better the writing becomes, because I learn how to put words together differently.

We practice every time we pick up a pen or a pencil or put our fingers on the keyboard. We practice being; we practice our trade. We don't need to be Shakespeare. We only need to be ourselves. We are the only one of us there is in this world. There's not another person like us, so no one can tell the world what we can, in the words we can. We have something valuable to offer. We are writers.

Facing the Blank Page

LH: My reaction to the blank page varies. Most of the time I want to get something on it so it's not blank anymore. All I am doing is getting words on the page. Some people think of writing as a terrible chore. I've never thought of it that way. Because I love writing, I don't care whether the page already has something on it or is blank. I can't wait to put words on it.

One reason why I don't edit as I write is because I don't want to spend time editing something that either is not where it belongs or may get thrown out altogether. A friend and I used to get together once a week to go over our poems. She gave excellent critiques. She would take almost every poem I wrote and say, "It's upside down." I'd have to switch the bottom with the top. She was right every single time. Because I never know, when I start, where the real beginning is, it usually turns out that I often write the end first.

CM: If I am ever intimidated by the blank page or by starting a project, that's when I'll work with a prompt. I'll set a timer and just put pen to paper in response to that prompt for a few minutes without interruption. By the end of that mini writing session, I usually feel more prepared to start my real project. I'm usually in the flow by then and feel excited about getting to it. Sometimes, I will force myself to just type a few words, any words, onto that blank page because what's in motion tends to stay in motion. A few words often lead to a few more words. Then the page isn't blank anymore. Not so scary after all.

Why We Like Prompts

CM: Writing with prompts invites me to think in ways that I wouldn't normally think, to explore topics and themes that I would tell you I had no interest in otherwise. They instruct my mind to shift focus and direction. I find that exciting. They can also be frustrating, of course. But even when the prompt is frustrating or uninteresting, in the beginning, I find that it helps to get my creative juices flowing. For me, prompts provide constraints, which I enjoy. I find them to be a valuable tool. I never know what worthwhile ideas or material might be generated from a simple writing prompt.

LH: I agree with Chloé. Prompts take me in directions I never would go otherwise. They make me think out of my own box, because I tend to write certain kinds of poems about certain topics. I keep doing them over and over, trying to get them to portray more clearly what it is I'm trying to say. If a prompt invites me to write about a piece of burnt toast, that would never have occurred to me. Once I receive the prompt, my mind goes on a different path to a different place. Sometimes I come up with something quite surprising that pleases me. I need expansion of what I know and what I understand to grow myself as a poet. I find that prompts do this. Some prompts are duds, no question, but interesting prompts carry me and my poems in new directions.

How to Use a Prompt

LH: I write prompts on slips of paper and keep them in a container. If I want to write a poem and have no idea what to write about, I pull out a prompt and take a journey with it. I accept the prompt no matter how peculiar it may seem. I don't have to like them. I just respond to them. A negative response can work well. I can do a little research if necessary, even if it never appears in the poem. When I received "Mamaluke sword" for a prompt, I had no idea what that was. I spent a lot of time chasing information about it online. It was fun. What came out was not at all what I expected. If I allow the prompt to lead, allow it to guide the journey, and choose unexpected words, I may open up new vistas.

CM: What she said! Above all else, play and enjoy.

Dealing with Inner Critics

CM: Many of us, I think, are familiar with that unfriendly, sometimes unrelenting, voice inside: "You said you were going to do that, and you didn't. You're such a loser. You're not a real writer. You can't even write a poem a day for a month?! What's wrong with you?" Listening to that kind of stuff is no fun, to say the least, and I really don't think that, in most cases, it does much to improve things. There are far better motivators than shame. If I shouldn't speak that way to someone else, then I shouldn't speak that way to myself.

I've come to learn that one's relationship with oneself as a writer, as an artist, as a human being, is essential. The only real constant in my life is me, and so developing a friendship with myself, learning how to speak to myself with love and kindness and compassion, can be critical skills to develop. How can we support ourselves, emotionally and spiritually, as writers? How can we cheer on that artist inside of us? How can we encourage, rather than discourage, our creativity and productivity? I think it's a wonderful thing when support and nurture can be rooted from within, as much as possible. Sometimes, of course, we need support from without to recognize our value within.

Inner critics are risk adverse. They don't want to see us get hurt, and so they often overestimate, in my opinion, the risks. They also tend to misrepresent them. Things can get distorted, and we can start to believe that what we're hearing is true when it's not.

If we can encourage ourselves and be rooted in our own inherent worth and dignity, if we can be our own cheerleader, then it might just become easier to say to our internal critics, and even our external critics, "Thank you, I hear you, and I am moving forward."

LH: I have more than one. I have a whole inner critic community. They have committee meetings frequently. It's difficult, because they're very loud and noisy, like Khrushchev when he banged his shoe on the table at the United Nations in 1960. They can be quite nasty. There are several different ways I deal with them. Sometimes I just say, "I hear you, thank you so much for telling me that, but right now I have to do something else. I won't forget that you told me that, I promise. I'm leaving now." Then I close the door on them. Sometimes that shuts them up.

The thing I've learned about inner critics, which almost everyone says, is they're just parts of ourselves that are scared we're going to get hurt. They're really trying to protect us. It sounds like an attack, it feels like an attack, but actually they're just trying to get us to stop doing something that might be scary or dreadful or have a bad outcome. Because they know everything bad that's ever happened to us from the day we were born, they don't want any of those things to happen to us again. Therefore, they're very watchful. They never sleep. They're always on their toes, and they can drive us crazy.

One thing to do is give them new jobs. "Thank you so much for taking care of that for me. Now I need you to do this. Would you mind, please, taking this boat over to Polynesia and counting how many pineapples there are on their trees? I need to know for this book I'm working on." It may help to give them fascinating, but very time-consuming jobs that are almost as hard as taking care of us.

They also have a tendency to worry about my getting too big a head. They have to prick the balloon periodically, so I don't get too set up with myself. They think, "You know, she's in for a fall if she doesn't stop this. We better take her down a peg." I can hear their pre-committee meeting. They say all kinds of things like, "Who do you think you are?" Most of what they say are lies. They're not lying on purpose. It's just that their understanding hasn't grown as I have grown. They still think of me as a little kid who needs to be protected from the world and life and everything horrible that might happen to me. I'm not a little kid anymore. I have to remind them and me I can take care of myself.

An Invitation

CM: We decided to call this book *Journey into Poetry*. At the start I think it was simply to refer to what we did together as a kind of fun, creative project, about the journey we took together, as writers and as friends. But through our discussions about what writing and poetry and creative expression can actually mean for a person, we agreed that we wanted to invite our readers to think about writing poetry.

We've included some prompts that might spark creative juices, to get people thinking about things they might not normally think about. Readers can make up their own prompts, too. It's all a fun experiment. To express oneself in poetry can be a powerful thing to do. We never know what might come from that.

If our readers are considering exploring poetry, I would suggest carving out some time each day—even just a few minutes—to work on poems. We are all so busy, and life is so hectic, that it can be so easy to push our creativity to the side. So maybe we're setting that alarm clock for a little bit earlier in the day or writing at the end of the night when things have quieted down, or maybe checking a prompt first thing in the morning, then thinking about it during the day and writing at night. However we find that time, we can figure out a way to commit to ourselves, and to writing a poem, perhaps one a week. See what comes up. Expect and anticipate with ease that a lot of it will not be perfect or even very good, and that's all okay.

Perhaps our readers know someone else who might want to take part, to be a poet companion, and to serve as a gentle accountability partner. I would encourage poets to invite someone else to journey into poetry with them. I can only speak for myself. It was so rewarding to do this with Lynn, with another poet, with someone who took me seriously more than she took the challenge seriously, if that makes sense. We had a really great time.

LH: I agree with Chloé. It was much more fun doing it with her than it was doing it by myself the previous year.

We poets have to write many words that don't work before we learn how to really put words together and become a wordsmith and a true poet. Every time we start a new project we are beginning from scratch. If we're writing a poem and going on a journey through the land of poetry, every station we get on or off teaches us something. Everyone we meet, everything we see, every time we say yes to the experience, we expand ourselves. We give the gift of attention to the things that feed our creativity. That grows us as creators and as human beings.

We learn new things. We have some tricks we've learned from the other stations where we've gotten on and off, but we may not be able to apply them. They may be totally useless, because at the new station there may be a whole different set of requirements. It's galvanizing to allow ourselves to really get submerged in what we'd love to do, because that way we learn all kinds of unusual things. We never know when we're going to need them, but everything that we learn is another little tool in our toolbox. Then, when a big opportunity comes, we've got all the tools we need to be able to produce the thing that we're being asked to create.

Some Prompts to Play With

If you'd like to experiment with prompts, here are some to get you started:

Lynn's favorite prompt: Grab the closest book. Go to any page. Refer to the 6th sentence and write down the next 12 words after it into a poem.

Chloé's favorite prompt:
Write a poem about a tea party you are having with your eleven-year-old self.

Write a poem:
— inspired by another line of poetry.
— about a family story.
— about a painting or photograph that you love.
— inspired by your least favorite holiday.
— about a vacation you've taken or long to take.
— inspired by your weekly grocery list.
— about the country of your birth.
— in the form of a prayer or meditation.
— only using words from a recent bill.
— about something physically or figuratively bigger than
    yourself.
— about how you are feeling right now.
— about someone or something you love.
— that explores the experience of loss.
— about your favorite celebration.
— about the process of change.
— about a time when you were sick.

— for children that rhymes.
— inspired by nature.
— of thanksgiving.
— to the phases of the moon.
— about weather in the form of a haiku.
— about water.
— to your favorite animal, in the form of a sonnet.
— to a friend.
— about your view at this moment.
— inspired by current events.
— about a memory you treasure.
— about television.
— about the value of work.
— to fear.
— about something that makes you laugh.
— inspired by the universe.
— to gratitude.
— about a place you call home.
— about longing.
— inspired by a historical figure.
— about war.
— inspired by music.
— from the perspective of a cat.
— about a wedding.
— to laundry.
— about your mother.
— to your favorite teacher.
— from the perspective of the desert.
— of thanksgiving to a cashier at a grocery store.
— about a cemetery.
— inspired by flight.
— about bedtime.
— to your inner child.
— that ends with the word "begin."
— to summer, in the form of a sonnet.

— from the perspective of the bully.
— about reconciliation.
— about misery.
— to ice cream, in the form of an ode.
— about a dream you have in your heart.
— inspired by sound.
— about the inner life of a Hawaiian bobtail squid.
— to an illness you've experienced.
— about the perfect gift.
— about "excellence."
— inspired by feeling shy.
— about being tired.
— about wandering and wondering.
— inspired by a book you love.
— about forgiveness.
— about being mistaken.
— about feeling forgotten.
— inspired by Beethoven's use of "Ode to Joy."
— about passion.
— about snow.
— to folly.
— from the perspective of an immigrant.
— to peace of mind.
— about a lazy poet.
— about elation.
— inspired by sleep.
— about exploration.
— from the perspective of a tortoise.
— inspired by a puddle.
— inspired by the poetry of Dorcas Watters,
      included in the Appendix.
— inspired by the third line of one of our poems.
— that includes a table, an apple, and a feather.
— about something that scares you.
— about a lobster lost at sea, in the form of a limerick.

— about maintaining perspective.
— about the life of a writer.
— about the life of a waiter.
— inspired by Vincent van Gogh's "The Night Café."
— to cancer.
— about trepidation.
— about birdsong.
— about your favorite cultural tradition.
— to nature.
— inspired by the hymn "Amazing Grace."
— about a yellow ribbon tied around an old tree.
— meant to convey a message of hope.
— of apology.
— about surrender.
— from the perspective of silence.
— about something you wish people understood about you.
— from the perspective of your favorite celebrity.
— that celebrates or denigrates food.
— about your funniest memory.
— that uses all five senses.

Write a poem inspired by the following poem, "Schooled (1962)", by Richard H. Fox.

This poem is about Cassie (Cassia) an orphan who lives on her grandfather Beeb's farm. In this poem, she is 11 years old.

Schooled (1962)

Cassie waves as the truck pulls in. School pickup.
Hiya Beeb. My teacher wants to see you. Now.
I'll stretch out in the bed and start my homework.

Beeb doesn't ask why.
His boots squeak as he crosses the green vinyl floor.
He knocks on the door, hears a weary voice. *Enter.*

He turns a chair around, folds his arms on the top rail.
Notes Teacher's stiff shoulders.
She puts a brass apple on a pile of papers.

Mr. Biebermann, we need to talk about Cassia.
She refuses to wear a dress for class photos.
All the other girls are matching colors and styles.

She insists on blue trousers with a plain white shirt.
I do not make exceptions for a girl's nonsense.
There is no good reason why she can't wear a dress.

Beeb cracks eight knuckles in one stretch.

Ma'am, Cassia's a farm girl, not like the other children.
Wakes before dawn, two hours of hard chores,
cleans up, fresh overalls, chow, comes to school.

She doesn't own a dress.
Weeding corn is an important task.
What she wears...foolishness.

Beeb plucks a burr off his sleeve.

I served as a Marine for ten years.
A Gunny knows the difference
between discipline and drivel.

Does Cassia complete assignments on time?
Does she participate courteously in class?
Does she address you with proper respect?

Teacher squints her eyes, exhales through her teeth.

Mr. Biebermann, I'm concerned about Cassia.
Other than the dress, her conduct is satisfactory.
She's a motivated student. Really, I do like her. Only—

she's so tall. Rough. Gorgeous hair,
but always tied back in a ponytail.
A trip to the beauty parlor—she'd be so pretty.

And her hands. Scars. Ragged nails.
She keeps to herself. Few friends.
Many classmates seem afraid of her.

Teacher spreads her fingers, pink polish.

Are there women in Cassia's life?
Relatives? Neighbors?
At the farm?

Beeb shakes his head no.

Mr. Biebermann, I suggest you find
a way for her to be among women.
I believe it would help her grow.

She'll learn feminine ways:
grooming, attire, deportment,
how to care for her body.

Beeb strokes his beard. Rips a burr from its bottom.

That's a very good suggestion, Ma'am.
I'm on it. But no dress for Cassia. I told her to be herself.

Who she is, who she'll be.
You might consider why she chooses
blue trousers and a white dress shirt.

- Richard H. Fox

Here are some possible prompts to play with:

Write a poem:
  — in narrative style.
  — that includes conversation.
  — about a time your parent interceded on your behalf at
     school.
  — about feeling different than your school classmates.
  — about a time when you felt a teacher was unfair to
     you.
  — to "blue trousers and a white dress shirt."

Write a poem inspired by the following poem, "I Am Turtle", by Jon Sebba.

I Am Turtle

for Chloé McFeters

I raise my scrawny head to Moon
wonder whether there is life after flood tide
I listen to breakers bellow imperatives.
Neptune thrusts his waves up the beach
I flee into foaming surf
I am Turtle. I beseech Moon.

If I could dive-bomb like pelicans
feel my body pierce the surface of rolling swells,
my wings caress a mermaid's scales
I'd worry whether warming will doom us,
whale and polar bear – no life after death.

I am Turtle. I appeal to Guardian Stars.
I know glaciers recede, oceans turn acid.
I want to scream, Turtles! Be ready for change.
I dream of an earth without people,
recovering from their damage. I only
hope my hatchlings can scrape out a future.
I pray to Tides. I am Turtle.

- Jon Sebba

Here are some possible prompts to play with:

Write a poem:
  — beginning I am.
  — from the point of view of an animal or a bird.
  — about climate change.
  — to a question you ponder.
  — from the perspective of change.
  — about recovering from damage.

Write a poem inspired by the following poem, "I Hear a Symphony", by Rochelle S. Cohen.

I Hear a Symphony

Black holes collide in the cosmos,
like cymbals crashing and punctuating
the dramatic climax of a symphony.
Ripples of gravitational waves then flow
across the fabric of space undetectable
to our senses but translated by ingenuity
to an audible sound akin to a bird's chirp.
A billion years after the collision,
we, the audience, awed and thrilled
by the distant song of space-time,
composer and conductor still unknown,
hear the momentary melody echoing
a concert performed an eternity ago.

- Rochelle S. Cohen

Here are some possible prompts to play with:

Write a poem:
    — about a sudden collision in the cosmos.
    — inspired by the origins of our existence.
    — about that which is "undetectable to our senses."
    — inspired by your particular field of knowledge.
    — about sound.
    — to the "composer and conductor."

Write a poem inspired by the following poem, "Greenwood Lake July 2019", by Eileen Van Hook.

Greenwood Lake
July 2019

Lunch on the lakeside terrace
on a glorious Sunday
the breeze off the water
lifts the paper placemats
the linen napkin on my lap
catches the beads of water
from my sweating glass
of raspberry iced tea
the french fries are dusted
with salt that clings to my lips
the crab cake tastes of
Cape Cod and happier times

I watch the sail boats glide
count the fuzzy new ducklings
along with my blessings
overhear the conversations
that surround our silent table
and it is almost enough.

- Eileen Van Hook

Here are some possible prompts to play with:

Write a poem:
— about a meal you remember.
— with sharp details using as many senses as possible.

— about a disappointment.
— that overhears a conversation.
— in which you count your blessings.
— to "almost enough."

Write a poem inspired by the following poem, "Louisiana Rain", by Louis H. Metoyer.

Louisiana Rain

I can hear the *tang tang* of
the drip drops down the gutter...

I can hear it go *pluck*
in a bucket...

I can hear a drop when it rolls
gently off a leaf and make a *pluck clup*...

I can hear it in the whistling winds
that bring chills to you as you lie awake,

hearing the *tap tap* of rain
against my windowpane.

- Louis H. Metoyer

Here are some possible prompts to play with:

Write a poem:
— where each stanza except the last begins with "I can hear".
— about the sounds of the rain where you live.
— about a chill that one cannot shake.
— about an afternoon spent indoors, waiting for the storm to
    pass.
— filled with the sounds of your house or yard.
— about noticing.

Other Ideas for Prompts

Many people subscribe to daily messages or read a daily meditation. Often those can be used as prompts.

Whatever you are reading, including junk mail, look for phrases, sentences, titles, that would be fun to play with.

Faith based writings offer rich prompts. Look at prayers or readings that speak to you. Is there a line that demands a poem?

Poems help process emotion. Love, loss, illness, death, change, insight, joy, and celebration are all fertile places from which to write poems.

Describe a favorite item of clothing in great detail: its appearance, feel, where and when you wore it, if someone gave it to you, how you felt when you wore it. Do you still have it? You can write about more than one item, maybe a series of poems.

Open a dictionary at random. Let your finger fall on a word. Do this five times. Use all five words as a prompt. Put them in a poem in any order.

Try your hand at different poetic forms:

      — rhymed or unrhymed poems
      — metered or unmetered poems
      — blank verse
      — free verse
      — limerick
      — anaphora
      — cinquain
      — acrostic
      — Shakespearean or Italian sonnet

— haiku
— ode
— cento
— pantoum
— narrative

For poets interested in the French forms (lai, triolet, rondel, rondeau, roundel, villanelle, ballade) we have included an excerpt of an essay, "Handbook of French Forms" by Dorcas Watters, Lynn's mother, in the Appendix. The essay contains rules for the various forms as well as examples written by her poet mother.

These are just a few forms – some formal, some not – with which poets play. If you try one that you enjoy, try using the form repeatedly until you really are comfortable with it. We invite you to keep your eyes and ears open for prompts. We think you will find them wherever you are.

In Conclusion

LH: I'd like to make a suggestion to our readers. Besides playing with prompts, I invite you to choose a poet you like, and immerse yourself in that poet's work for maybe a month. Read. Reread. Use a line or two from that poet as a prompt or attempt to write in a similar style. Then move on to another poet. The more good poetry we read, the better poets we will become.

What I hope our readers take away from our book is that it's okay to be who we are. Whatever comes into our head is something to put on paper. We can allow the writing to be itself. It won't ever be perfect, but it will say what needs to be said. It might say the things the poet knows that maybe no one else knows.

Something we say, and we will rarely know what it is, may save somebody's life, not necessarily physically, maybe emotionally, maybe mentally. We have no way to know how our writing is going to affect other people. When we put our writing out in the world, we have to let the writing do its work. We are done. We're out of the picture. Now the interchange is going to be between our poetry and the reader. The reader always brings something to the reading. The reader is co-creating with the poem that they're reading. They're taking from it what they need to get from it. It may not be at all what we thought we said, but it's what they need. That's what's important. The best we can do is the best we can do. After that we have to let our babies grow up, be themselves, and keep our sticky fingers off them.

CM: I hope people take away that if *we* could do this, then they can certainly do this. We can do this together! We can banish or befriend our fear enough to just get started. We can write poetry, even if we've never done it before.

Our unique overview of this wondrous world that we live in, and of our experience as part of it, is something that we've earned. Our stories have value to others out there. No one can take that away from us, not even if they try really hard. There might be voices out there, opinions coming from family or friends, or strangers online, that might not be so kind or caring. Maybe they even sound worse than our own Inner Critic. It can be difficult to receive critical opinions and comments, because when we're writers, or artists — when we are human — rejection or criticism can feel personal, even when it isn't.

But I would say it's important to remember that those voices and opinions are not the only voices and opinions out there. People are entitled to their tastes. We just have to remember that other people's tastes are what they bring to how they read our work, and oftentimes, that has so little to do with us.

So, instead, I might try to focus on the people out there who need to hear what you have to say, who will not only need it, but will love it. There are people out there who might be made happier by our writing and who will maybe even be comforted, helped, or healed by it. That is a gift that I hope we don't keep to ourselves if we're considering writing and sharing our work. There are people out there who are there to support us and encourage us. If we haven't found those people yet, we keep looking, because they are out there. Just like Lynn was out there and the other wonderful souls in the group we joined.

I also hope that people who read this book will remember that we don't need to take ourselves so seriously. It's okay to have fun and do something imperfectly just because it brings us joy. Not all writing, poetry, art has to be "serious" to be meaningful or powerful or affecting. At least I don't think so. Please take away that writing can be fun. And that we all are already creative beings simply because we are human. So, embrace your gifts, share your voice, and most importantly, enjoy your unique journey.

Appendix

Note from Lynn: My mother, Dorcas Watters, was a fine poet. I didn't discover my inner poet until late in life. My mother was always a poet and identified as a poet. Formal poetry was her natural language. Because the French forms intrigued her, she wrote this essay to encourage others to play with them.

Handbook of French Forms

by Dorcas Watters

The French forms are fixed poem patterns which have travelled a long way and a long time, from medieval France, to reach us. They have an honorable ancestry, beginning with the troubadours of Provence. Some of their makers were upper-class and some were ignoble, but being poets, they all took part in the nobility of creation.

The rules for the writing of these fixed French forms were codified in a book in 1403. Chaucer and his contemporaries imported the forms to England. Many poets have an occasional serious poem in this genre; Robinson's "House on the Hill" is a villanelle, as is Dylan Thomas's "Do not go gentle into that good night." However, generally speaking, in modern usage, these poetic forms are given to light verse. It takes considerable practice to feel at home in them. To a poet, whose thoughts must flow, these forms are as constricting as shoes to normally bare feet. They are excellent to use as practice, being very difficult to do well, since they have so few rhyming sounds and a refrain which must be made to recur with seeming naturalness.

The lai is a very early form. It turns on two rhymes: a, a, b, a, a, b, a, a, b. The "a" lines have five syllables (not feet); the "b" lines have two syllables. There is no fixed number of lines for a stanza. If the poem has more than one stanza, each stanza has its own set of rhyme sounds. Here is an example:

Lai

Velvet, the night came;
Royal, a right frame
For you.
Virgo, a light name,
The star, the bright flame,
Pierced through.
Charmed and my fright tame,
I could not quite claim
My due.

The triolet belongs to the rondeau family. It is an eight-line stanza with two rhymes, the first and second lines being used also as the seventh and eighth; the first line being used as the fourth. Thus the pattern (the capital letters representing repeated lines) is: A, B, a, A, a, b, A, B. The lines may have ten, eight, or six syllables. The first of these triolets is regular; the other two have variations. The idea helps mold the form and very often will not be cramped in it. This, of course, is the prime difficulty with the French forms, and the reason why they are not more often used for serious work, as well as their challenge and their pleasure.

Sassy

Sassy, my Siamese,
Left broken crockery.
She was a cruel tease,
Sassy, my Siamese.
Now that she's gone, she's
Made my love mockery.

Sassy, my Siamese,
Left broken crockery.

Caribbean

I listened to the surf instead;
I never wrote my triolet.
I watched the preening bird and read
Contentment from the surf instead,
And saw the palm tree bend his head
Where sun and wind and water met.
I listened to the surf instead
And never wrote my triolet.

Thanks to a Stranger

Like a blackbird you whistled me
     Into the summer day.
Just knowing how to be,
Like a blackbird, you whistled me
Out of myself and free.
     Surprised, on your flowery way,
Like a blackbird you whistled me
     Into the summer day.

The rondel was the form which Charles D'Orleans (1394-1456) perfected. It consists of thirteen lines of any length built on two rhymes and a refrain. The pattern is A, B, b, a; a, b, A, B; a, b, b, a, A. The first of these runs relatively true to the pattern; the second is a variation.

Tap Dance

Music sets her heel
     Taping on the floor.

She cannot wait for more,
Whether waltz or reel.

Having the appeal
      Of an open door,
Music sets her heel
      Taping on the floor.

She has known it steal
      Boredom from a bore,
      Give her wings to soar.
Where ego learns to kneel
Music sets her heel.

Capriccio

The horn is piercing sweet–
      The soft rush of the strings
      Like flickering, airy wings
Goes up and up to meet,
In a windy, far retreat,
      The gold, the flute upflings.
The horn is piercing sweet.
      The soft rush of the strings
      Like fountain-water clings
To air, and shines. Though fleet
This bubble world, complete
      As victory, it sings.
The horn is piercing sweet.

The rondeau is one of the most popular of the French forms. "In Flanders Field" is a poem in this form. There are fifteen lines, any meter and any length. The first part of the first line is used as the refrain. Thus (with R standing for refrain) the pattern is: Ra, a, b, b, a; a, a, b, R; a, a, b, b, a, R.

When I Am Gone

When I am gone, the spring will still come in
With raindrops hammering lustily on tin
    Rooftops and brawling birds and skates,
    And boys and girls with spring-bemuséd pates
Will eat and still be hungry and grow thin.

The red flowers of the maple will begin,
The rioting frogs create their merry din,
    The brooks will roister in their white foam-spates,
        When I am gone.

And may there be some quiet girl to pin
A hopeful lilac in her hair, her skin
    As cool and fragrant, and these lilac mates,
    Sitting in silence, may the opening gates
Of living and of loving their faith win,
        When I am gone.

The roundel, a variation on the rondeau, was invented by Swinburne. It has eleven lines in three stanzas. The refrain is the first word, or first few words of line one and this usually rhymes with line two. Therefore the pattern is: Ra, b, a, R(b); b, a, b; a, b, a, R (b).

The Little Rain

The little rain reminded me
Of a song I'd sung in pain,
When I had almost desired to be
    The little rain.

When I had tears for a refrain
And missing you was more to me
Than I could ever endure again.

O westryn wind, that passion's plea
Wore, in my nerves, its winding lane.
Tonight, it wakes old agony,
          The little rain.

The villanelle, which was originally a "round song taken up by men on a farm" (villa) was a pastoral to accompany a rustic dance. Therefore it has a regular system of repeated lines. The early form was loose. One of Jean Passerat's (d. 1602) posthumous villanelles became so popular that it set the standard for all following ones. This form has nineteen lines of any meter and length. It is arranged in six stanzas: five of three lines each, the sixth of four lines. The first and third lines of the first stanza are used as the refrain. The pattern is: R1a, b, R2a; a, b, R1a; a, b, R2a; a, b, R1a; a, b, R2a; a, b, R1a, R2a.

Ring Around

They said I must be true
And never led astray,
But what did they tell you?

I kept my longings few;
Resolved I would obey;
They said I must be true.

The not impossible who
Came wandering by one day,
But what did they tell you?

124

A kiss would hardly do,
Though if I'd had my way–
They said I must be true.

Yet something was his due.
I owed. I had to pay.
But what did they tell you?

You found another too?
You cad! How dare you, pray?
They said I must be true,
But what did they tell you?

The ballades are a different family from the same parent stem. They are much longer. Because they are more spacious, they are easier to write. The poet can set up an idea, play with it, or develop it, and bring it to a conclusion in the envoy (a summation or dedication ending the poem). The prime difficulty is in choosing rhyme words, especially for the "b" rhymes, which have enough matching rhyme words to carry the poet to the end. As in other French forms, as used in English verse, no rhyme sound may be repeated even though the sense and spelling are different. For instance, *bare* and *forebear* may not rhyme with *bear*.

The ballade is the oldest of French forms. The earlier ballades have no envoy, but by Chaucer's time this had been added. In the three stanzas of eight lines each, the rhyme scheme must be identical: a, b, a, b, b, c, b, C and the refrain b, c, b, C.

The Warning

Spun silver edged the lilac flower
        Lifting a dazzled, fragrant head;
A sleepless night was springtime's dower,

"Love him," were all the words she said.
  My spirit, softly, stainless led,
From its poor husk had just got free
  When I saw dawn creep to my bed—
Through windy fields the shadows flee.

The sun burst up, with gorgeous power,
  A scourge to night's remotest dread,
Who taught the darkest imps to cower
  And woke the winter's purest dead;
  Yet, with my living flesh half fed,
The twilight vanquished him and he
  Absconded with my vital bread—
Through windy fields the shadows flee.

The feast was laid in a frosty hour;
  The earth to death was being wed;
I saw the hills, a purple bower,
  With dauntless joy the board was spread.
  I looked for tears, but found instead
Laughter and caroling, all mad glee.
  "Mirth!" World-wide the message sped—
Through windy fields the shadows flee.

Thou foolish one, though trees flaunt red,
  Disdaining weak mortality,
Remember they are being bled—
  Through windy fields the shadows flee.

Sometimes the ballade has a ten-line stanza, in which case there are four rhymes instead of three. A variation is the ballade with the double refrain; one refrain being the fourth line of each stanza; the other being the eighth.

The Maze

Once, I remember, joy
    Shimmered on all my days.
Where is the pretty toy?
    Love is an endless maze
    With innumerable ways
Of making brilliance bright,
    Piling blaze on blaze—
Better not think tonight.

Peace without alloy,
    The gentleness of haze
Then brightness starts to cloy:
    Love is an endless maze
    Of mystery – with bays
For its defeated. Fright
    It soothes, and hope? It frays—
Better not think tonight.

Stern, and it can destroy.
    Sometimes it turns and flays
A reckless, headstrong boy.
    Love is an endless maze,
    And though I know it slays
Even Daphne in her flight,
    Yet, I have sung its praise—
Better not think tonight.

O foolish song I raise—
    Love is an endless maze
Of hate and hurt, and light—
    Better not think tonight.

A poet must have some kind of container in which to pour his material. Without form, the material is void, an amorphous mass. Children make poems with mud pies. No amount of tumbling words will make a poem unless they are shaped to some design. Even free verse is not free from this necessity. Amy Lowell's "Patterns" has as true a shape as any sonnet. However, often the material dictates its own form, as cement makes sidewalks and blown glass vases. Most poets, I think, work from the material to the form as a sculptor cuts away the excrescence of stone to reveal the hidden statue.

Working with the French forms is, in a sense, a backward job. Instead of finding the form that suits the material, one clips one's material to fit the form. Nevertheless, for an aspiring poet, working with the French forms is excellent practice, as arpeggios are for an aspiring musician. If these forms are practiced enough, so that they become habitual, part of the poet's normal equipment, so to speak, they can make sweet and serious music.

About the Authors

Lynn Hoins

Lynn Hoins, poet, published in journals including *Earth's Daughters*, *Inkwell*, *Chronogram*, and *cine sera*, has two chapbooks published by Finishing Line Press: *You Were Always Music* and *Called by Stones*. Forthcoming a new chapbook, *Walking with the Tiger*. Also forthcoming, her memoir, working title *Letters to My Father*. She taught poetry workshops for The College of Poetry of The Northeast Poetry Center, Warwick, New York. She features and reads at open mics in New York State and Utah. Learn more at www.lynnhoins.com.

Chloé McFeters

Chloé McFeters is a writer, coach, consultant, documentarian, and a published poet. Her documentary film, *You Look a Lot Like Me*, explores the issue of relationship violence and is used as an educational and training resource in a variety of settings across the U.S. She is the author of more than a dozen guided coloring book journals for adults exploring a range of experiences, including living with cancer, family caregiving, and women's military service. You can often find her wandering around a local library, bookshop, or botanical garden. Learn more at www.chloemcfeters.com.

About the Contributors

Richard H. Fox

Richard Fox seeks three-decker rainbows, fluent scout dogs, and illuminating espresso. When not writing about rock 'n roll or youthful transgressions, his poems focus on cancer from the patient's point of view drawing on hope, humor, and unforeseen gifts.

He is the author of four poetry collections: *Time Bomb* (2013), *wandering in puzzle boxes* (2015), *You're my favorite horse* (2017), *embracing the burlesque of collateral damage* (2020) plus a chapbook: *The Complete Uncle Louie Poems* (2017).

The new collection, *embracing the burlesque of collateral damage,* features a braided narrative: a novella in verse "Cassie at Beeb's Farm" with parallel poems that reflect the poet's life and dreams.

The winner of the 2017 Frank O'Hara Prize, Richard seconds Stanley Kunitz' motion that people in Worcester are "provoked to poetry." Learn more at www.smallpoetatlarge.com.

Rochelle S. Cohen

Dr. Rochelle S. Cohen, is the author of the recently released poetry book *Ode for the Time Being*. Dr. Cohen was born in Brooklyn, New York. She is presently Professor Emerita at the University of Illinois at Chicago, where she was the recipient of the 2008 College of Medicine at Chicago Distinguished Faculty Award. She is a neuroscientist with publications in synaptic structure and biochemistry and hormonal effects on brain and behavior. She was recently Guest Associate Co-Editor with Dr. Alberto Rasia-Filho and Dr. Oliver von Bohlen of a Special Issue and e-book of *Frontiers in Psychiatry: Frontiers in Synaptic Plasticity: Dendritic Spines, Circuitry and Behavior*.

The poems in *Ode for the Time Being* reflect Dr. Cohen's life-long passion for marine life and science, as well as her deep love for her late husband, the writer and artist Rex Sexton.

Eileen Van Hook

Eileen Van Hook's work has been published in various journals and anthologies. She placed first in a poetry contest in "The Writer", has been recognized three times in the Allen Ginsberg Poetry Contest (once in Second Place) and is a two-time Pushcart Prize nominee. Eileen lives and writes in the wilds of northwestern New Jersey.

Jon Sebba

Jon Sebba, a retired engineer, lives in Salt Lake City and Tucson. He fought in the 1967 Arab-Israeli War. A collection of his poems, mostly from the POV of a frontline soldier, was awarded the 2013 Utah State Poetry Society Book of the Year. He writes to witness all aspects of life, including social and environmental injustice. He still writes about the lingering impacts of war in the hope that, as more people understand the truth about combat, fewer will support it.

Louis H. Metoyer

Louis H. Metoyer was born in Natchitoches, Louisiana, and is a proud member of the Cane River Creole community. From a very young age, growing up in his close-knit parish, Louis was instilled with a deep appreciation for his family, his heritage, and his unique culture. For the past 30 years, Louis has served as the founder, executive director, and editor of his family's celebrated grass-roots publication, The Bayou Talk Newspaper. He is a writer, artist, and educator and the author of two poetry collections, *Creole* and *Within My Thoughts*. Learn more at www.louishmetoyer.com.

Stephen T. Vessels

Stephen T. Vessels is a professional editor and Thriller Award nominated author of SF, dark fantasy and cross-genre fiction. His stories have appeared in Ellery Queen Mystery Magazine, the Santa Barbara Literary Journal, collections from Borda Books, Grey Matter Press, ShadowSpinners and others. *The Mountain & The Vortex and Other Tales*, a collection of some of his stories, is available from Muse Harbor Publishing. His novels, *The Door of Tireless Pursuit* and *The Ruptured Firmament* were released by ShadowSpinners Press. He has written art and music reviews for the Santa Barbara Independent and is a published poet and a visual artist. An exhibit of his ballpoint pen drawings was exhibited at the Andre Zarre Gallery in Manhattan Chelsea, New York City, throughout August 2016.

Chris Wozney

Chris Wozney spent most of a semi-idyllic childhood reading avidly against a musical background of the classical music, opera, and Broadway recordings her parents loved, with access to multi-generational family libraries that contained a great deal of children's literature, poetry, comparative religion, and philosophy. Growing up, she aspired to be a mix of Dickon, d'Artagnan, and Cyrano de Bergerac. Chris actually enjoyed learning how to diagram sentences in 5th grade, and her favorite part of editing is discerning when to employ rules to serve the story or the narrative voice, and when and how and why to go around the rules. She spent 4 years as an Army medic during a quieter part of Desert Storm. Since 1999 she has divided time primarily between family, teaching, learning tai chi, writing book reviews, filking, and editing.

Dorcas Watters

Dorcas Watters [1911-1990] was a poet, gifted teacher, and extraordinary parent to Lynn Hoins. She describes her life in the poem "The Score."

I've done most things in my life: ridden on the back of a motorcycle – the delicious lean and lift, walked on the wet sand and pushed my toes in deep, been bouleversé by the frigid waves of Maine, felt the small plane lift with its organ bars under my feet, found love, lost love, found love, lost love – the rhythm of the years, seen the Pieta unglassed and Breughel, Goya, Magritte, danced until dawn, heard the sweet call of Bach's *Komm Susser Tod*, held books, drunk in the seasons – oh, the anise smell of fields of devil's paint brush, had a home and kittens and a child, and losses like a bottomless black tarn. Counting it up, I've had a world and wealth.

Thank You

Thank you so much for your purchase of our poetry book, *Journey into Poetry.*

If you enjoyed our little collection, **please consider leaving a short review online wherever you purchased your copy.** This helps other people discover the book too, as well as the wonderful work of some of the other writers and poets featured herein.

Sherman Point Press is able to offer scaled discounts to book clubs, schools, universities, and non-profit organizations. Please contact sales@shermanpoint.com for more information and for assistance with placing your bulk order.

Made in United States
North Haven, CT
25 October 2021